D1348797

3 8002 02242 897 5

**Coventry
City Council**

CCS

3 8002 02242 897 5

Askews & Holts	Oct-2015
J338.761647 JUNIOR N	£12.99

big brands

McDONALD'S

Cath Senker

WAYLAND

contents

The Golden Arches — 4

McDonald's is born — 6

McDonald's across the world — 8

The fast-food revolution — 10

"In business for yourself but not by yourself" — 12

Bringing in the children — 14

Big brand tie-ins — 16

McDonald's and the products discussed in this book are either trademarks or registered trademarks of the McDonald's Corporation. This is not an official publication of McDonald's, and the views set out herein are solely those of the author.

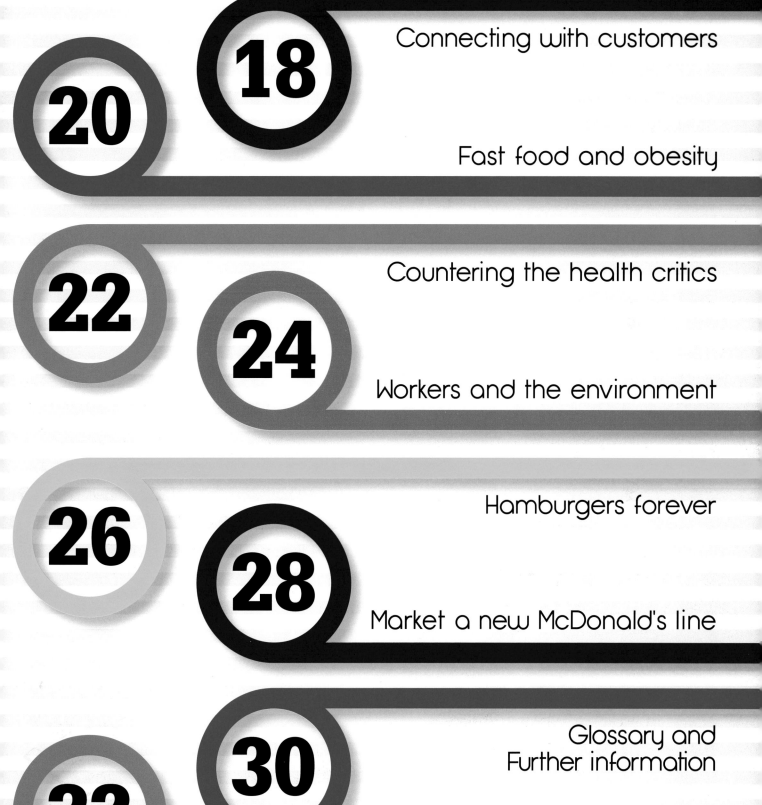

18 Connecting with customers

20 Fast food and obesity

22 Countering the health critics

24 Workers and the environment

26

28 Hamburgers forever

Market a new McDonald's line

30 Glossary and
Further information

32 Index

the golden arches

McDonald's in Tel Aviv, Israel, serves kosher food – prepared to suit religious Jews.

Business Matters
Diversification

In business, diversifying means adapting to different markets. McDonald's knows that Japanese customers don't eat as much as Americans, so the burger you buy in Kyoto is smaller than the one you'd buy in Kansas.

If you find yourself in any major city in the world, the chances are that you'll soon spot a McDonald's restaurant. McDonald's is the biggest fast-food chain on the planet, with sales of more than US $13 billion in 2013, over 34,000 outlets and 1.8 million employees.

McDonald's core products are its classic burgers, shakes and fries. You could eat a McDonald's cheeseburger anywhere in the world and it would taste the same. Yet as well as offering its regular fare, McDonald's also caters to local preferences because more than half of its restaurants are outside the USA. In Brazil, you can buy a Quiche de Queijo (cheese quiche), the Red Bean Pie is available in Hong Kong, and in India, there are plenty of vegetarian options.

This book examines how founder Ray Kroc built McDonald's from a single burger restaurant into a global chain with branches across the world, and into one of the best-known brands worldwide. Although going to McDonald's is a hugely popular treat, the company has met with criticism for fuelling obesity. If you eat a Big Mac and large fries with a large coke, you'll consume 1,430 calories – more than half the daily recommended amount for an adult – and 59g of fat – twice the recommended daily amount. In this book, we consider what McDonald's is doing about this, and how likely it is to stay at the top of the fast-food market.

North America

Europe

Asia

South America

Africa

Australia

⬭ Countries with McDonald's

⬭ Countries without McDonald's

A 2011 map showing countries with and without McDonald's. Much of Africa has no McDonald's restaurants.

Building the Brand

Brand recognition

Four out of five children recognize the McDonald's Golden Arches logo by the time they are three years old – before some of them even know their own surnames.

McDonald's is born

I In the USA in the 1940s, as the numbers of car owners rose, drive-in restaurants became all the rage. Drivers parked, and female 'carhops' served them in their vehicles. In 1948, Mac and Dick McDonald opened their McDonald's drive-in in San Bernardino, California, providing speedy self-service and cheap burgers. It was hugely popular.

In 1954, salesman Ray Kroc was delighted to receive an order from McDonald's for eight multi-mixers for making milkshakes. When Kroc visited, he found that McDonald's burgers sold for about half the regular price. Owing to the self-service counter, there was no need to employ carhops. The food was ready-cooked, wrapped and kept warm under heat lamps so it could be served quickly.

The McDonald brothers weren't interested in expanding the business. But Kroc pitched his big idea to set up McDonald's restaurants all over the USA. Mac and Dick agreed – for a fee. In 1955 Kroc founded the McDonald's Corporation and opened his first restaurant in Des Plaines, Illinois. It offered a basic menu of just nine items including hamburgers, fries and shakes. Workers made the food on an assembly line, producing burgers that looked and tasted exactly the same.

The business grew rapidly; in 1958 the company sold its millionth hamburger. Four years later, the first McDonald's restaurant with indoor seating opened in Denver, Colorado, and by 1965, more than 700 McDonald's restaurants dotted the USA.

Business Matters
Pricing tactics

Companies may offer a new product at a lower price than their competitors to win sales – Ray Kroc sold his burgers for the bargain price of 15 cents (about 10p today). This pricing strategy is called penetration.

The McDonald Brothers' original restaurant in San Bernadino, California.

Ray Kroc
McDonald's founder, president and chair (1955–84)

Ray Kroc was an ambitious businessman – from early on, he said that he intended to open 1,000 McDonald's restaurants. The secret of his business model was offering food of consistently high quality, good service and a clean environment. For example, the hamburger meat had to be exactly centred on the bun, and the restaurant facilities, especially the toilets, had to be spotless.

> **If I had a brick for every time I've repeated the phrase Quality, Service, Cleanliness and Value, I think I'd probably be able to bridge the Atlantic Ocean with them.**
>
> Ray Kroc, *Grinding It Out*, 1977

Customers at Ray Kroc's first McDonald's in Des Plaines, Illinois in 1955.

McDonald's across the world

Kroc developed the McDonald's look so his restaurants would be instantly recognizable. In 1969, the bright yellow Golden Arches logo was made more prominent and became the key symbol of McDonald's.

The original menu was expanded to bring in more customers. In 1975, McDonald's restaurant owner Herb Peterson of Santa Barbara, California invented the Egg McMuffin to entice people to have breakfast at McDonald's. A clever marketing manager thought, 'Why not have a meal just for children?' and in 1979, Happy Meals were born. When children opened the box, they found a toy nestled in with their burger, fries and cookies.

McDonald's went international, too. In 1967, branches opened in Canada and Puerto Rico, and by 1983 there were McDonald's restaurants in 32 countries.

A McDonald's Happy Meal in its bright, appealing box.

Building the Brand
Giving to the community

Russians queue up on the day that McDonald's opened in Moscow.

Business Matters
Logos and slogans

Companies devise logos and slogans and use them across all their stores and publicity so consumers recognize them instantly. The McDonald's Golden Arches logo and the slogan 'i'm lovin' it' are among the best known in the world.

As Communism fell in Eastern Europe, McDonald's was seen as a symbol of the Western lifestyle. On the day that the first McDonald's opened in Moscow, Russia in 1990, more than 30,000 customers queued up for burgers!

Yet in the late 20th century, the company expanded too quickly. In 2002, McDonald's made a loss for the first time. As Chief Executive Officer Jim Skinner noted, this was the year of the 'perfect storm', when everything went wrong. McDonald's had been opening 2,000 stores a year, an unmanageable level of growth that had resulted in a lack of attention to basics. Customers complained about dirty stores, cold food and unfriendly staff. Skinner's strategy was to slow down growth and improve the existing stores, focusing on cleanliness and efficient service. The kitchens were revamped, and food was made fresh to order. More chicken and salad dishes were introduced to provide healthier options.

It is good for a business's image to undertake charity work, and Kroc wanted to show that McDonald's gave back to communities. In 1974, the first Ronald McDonald House opened, a charity offering free accommodation for families with children in hospital. As of 2014, there were houses in 62 countries around the world – including this one in the Netherlands.

the fast-food revolution

Young people enjoying malt drinks at a US café in the 1950s

McDonald's achieved success because it started out in the right place at the right time. After World War II (1939–45), a new fast-food culture developed in Western countries. Economies were expanding, wages were rising and more people had cars. They had leisure time and money to spend, so going out to eat became a favourite treat. Fast-food chains such as McDonald's, Burger King and Kentucky Fried Chicken grew rapidly.

The industry was revolutionized by innovation in food preparation technology. Assembly-line production was introduced so skilled chefs were not required – each worker in the line followed strict instructions to do one task, such as frying the burger patties. Many of the customers bought take-away food and did not use the restaurant facilities, reducing the company's costs further. Self-service fast-food outlets put many traditional restaurants out of business.

Chains such as McDonald's and Burger King were family friendly – cheerful, bright and air-conditioned, with clean toilets. They also proved popular with workers eating alone; burgers and fries made a cheap, quick meal for lunch breaks.

The restaurants spread quickly owing to the franchising system. McDonald's was one of the leaders in introducing franchising, in which owner/operators purchased the restaurants and ran them. Franchising used the benefits of the company's management and systems, and linked them to local businesspeople who invested their own money in the restaurants.

> **While the Company's menu is limited, it contains food staples [basics] that are widely accepted in North America. It is for these reasons that demand for its products is less sensitive to economic fluctuations [changes] than most other restaurant formats.**
>
> **Ray Kroc explains why fast-food restaurants are so popular, 1977**

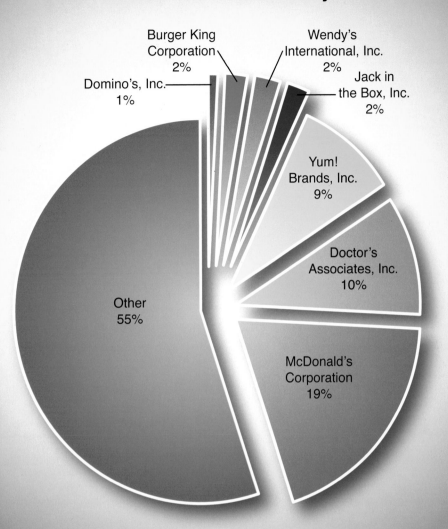

Market Shares of the Major Players in the Fast-Food Industry

Burger King Corporation
2%

Wendy's International, Inc.
2%

Domino's, Inc.
1%

Jack in the Box, Inc.
2%

Yum! Brands, Inc.
9%

Doctor's Associates, Inc.
10%

Other
55%

McDonald's Corporation
19%

A 2012 chart showing the market shares of companies in the US fast-food industry.

A waitress takes orders at an early drive-through restaurant.

Business Matters
Product life cycle

Every product goes through these stages: introduction, growth, maturity and decline. As products decline, they are withdrawn and new ones are introduced – this is the product life cycle. According to McDonald's, the Big Mac is probably at the 'maturity' stage.

"In business for yourself but not by yourself"

Kroc built McDonald's on the principle of the 'three-legged stool' – the McDonald's Corporation, the franchisees and the suppliers together were the key to success. He told franchisees that '[you are] in business for yourself, but not by yourself.'

Most McDonald's restaurants are run under the franchise system. Today, there are more than 3,000 owner/operators in the USA. If you're thinking of setting up as a US franchisee, you'll need a minimum investment of around US $750,000 – and 25 per cent ($187,500) has to be paid up front (the rest can be borrowed). So you need to be quite wealthy to begin with! McDonald's focuses on countries where it already has restaurants and keeps a list of countries where

Coffee is served at a McCafé outlet in Illinois, USA.

Business Matters
Training

Companies train their staff to work according to the business's standards. In 1961, McDonald's opened Hamburger University, at Elk Grove Village, Illinois, to instruct franchisees and operators how to run a McDonald's restaurant.

One of more than 60 McDonald's restaurants in Miami, USA.

it is seeking franchisees. You'll need to check if your country is one of them.

The franchisees all have to follow McDonald's core values of quality, service, cleanliness and value. But they are free to develop their own ideas to improve the business. It was franchisees who came up with the Big Mac, the Filet-O-Fish and the Egg McMuffin.

Although individuals run the branches, all McDonald's products must be identical everywhere. For example, all suppliers making a cheeseburger have to match a target product. All the ingredients, such as the seasonings, are tested and tasted, with testers making notes after every bite. If the taste doesn't match the target, the supplier has to try again until it does.

Fred Turner
Head of Operations, 1957–68

Fred Turner was always thinking of ways to make the McDonald's operation faster. He asked bakers to provide individual burger buns already sliced all the way through, rather than in clusters of four or six. Turner wrote the McDonald's handbook, which gave every detail of all McDonald's production methods. For instance, French fries had to be cut precisely 0.7 cm (0.28 in) thick. He also pushed for franchisees to be involved in running stores rather than just investing in them – a very successful strategy.

Fred Turner rose from burger flipper to the top of McDonald's.

bringing in the children

A nother key to McDonald's success is the way it attracts children to its restaurants. In the USA, children aged 2 to 11 see more than twice the number of McDonald's adverts than those of its competitors.

Children are an easy target; research shows that children under eight generally do not realize that an advert is trying to sell them something. They believe what they see is true. McDonald's adverts tell them that Happy Meals are perfect for children, so they may ask their parents to take them to McDonald's.

It's the toys that are the major attraction of Happy Meals though. A successful toy promotion can double or triple the number of children's meals McDonald's sells in a week. Often, McDonald's distributes a set of toys so children make repeat visits to collect them all.

When challenged about marketing high-fat fast food to children, McDonald's replies that it promotes healthy options in its adverts for children, focusing on fruit, vegetables and milk. The restaurants sell more of these items than ever before.

> " The restaurant chain [McDonald's] evoked a series of pleasing images in a youngster's mind: bright colours, a playground, a toy, a clown, a drink with a straw, little pieces of food wrapped up like a present. "
>
> Eric Schlosser, *Fast Food Nation*, 2001

Ha
Meal
are o
charac
f
popu
mov

Business Matters
Marketing directly to children

Encouraging children to eat fast food is a successful marketing strategy because food preferences are formed during the first few years of life. It's been shown that children who eat Happy Meals are more likely to become frequent adult visitors to McDonald's than those who don't.

Building the Brand
Ronald McDonald

In the 1960s, the McDonald's marketing team decided the company needed a child-friendly character to attract young visitors, and put huge efforts into creating the Ronald McDonald clown. In 1966 Ronald appeared in his first national TV advert. With his bright appearance and friendly personality, he proved an instant hit. He continues to represent the brand to this day, and McDonald's claims Ronald McDonald is the most recognizable character on the planet, second only to Santa!

Getting into the football spirit at the McDonald's World Cup launch party, New York, USA, 2014.

Business Matters

Marketing alliances

A marketing alliance is an agreement between two companies to promote each other's products.

big brand tie-ins

Popular children's characters Woody and Buzz Lightyear deliver Happy Meals at McDonald's in Tokyo, Japan.

McDonald's has often made marketing alliances with other big brands to encourage customers to link a favourite drink, activity or sport with its food.

Since 1955, McDonald's has had a marketing agreement with Coca-Cola to sell its drinks in all McDonald's outlets. Burgers, fries and Coke make a perfect combination, which is highly profitable for both companies – about 5 per cent of McDonald's profits come from the sale of soft drinks. However, the burger giant has been criticized for selling large cup sizes of sugary drinks with its meals.

In 1996, McDonald's made a ten-year global marketing agreement with entertainment giant Disney. McDonald's outlets opened at Disney theme parks, and children were excited to find toys linked to the latest Disney movie in Happy Meals. This was a clever marketing ploy. McDonald's knew that parents took their children to McDonald's because they wanted to feel like good parents and make the kids happy – and it was far cheaper than visiting a Disney theme park. The adverts proclaimed, 'Only McDonald's makes it easy to get a bit of Disney magic.' But Disney refused to renew the deal in 2006, preferring to distance itself from fast food because of the dramatic rise in obesity.

McDonald's links with high-profile sports events continue though. During the 2014 World Cup, McDonald's GOL! programme ('gol' means 'goal' in Portuguese) asked 12 artists from around the world to create football-related designs on fries boxes. Customers could hold their mobile phone to the box to download an app with an augmented reality game involving 'kicking' a ball by flicking a finger.

Roy Bergold
Chief Creative Officer (c. 1972–2001)

Faced with falling sales in the early 2000s, McDonald's hoped to rebuild the emotional link people felt with the company, reminding them of how they'd loved McDonald's in the past. Roy Bergold was in charge of the marketing campaign, writing that 'The challenge of the campaign is to make customers believe that McDonald's is their "Trusted Friend".' The company made alliances with other big brands, such as Disney, so that customers would associate enjoyable events with McDonald's and feel that the company knew their needs and cared about them.

connecting with customers

Just as McDonald's marketing alliances create a positive image of the brand, its direct marketing to customers focuses on their feelings, so when they arrive hungry in a new city, the idea of McDonald's pops straight into their heads.

Customers clearly do link fast food with the McDonald's brand. In 2014, it was the top fast-food brand in the list of most valuable global brands compiled by BrandZ (a company that ranks the world's leading brands).

Yet McDonald's cannot rely on its brand reputation alone, and uses all kinds of media to spread its message. Online, it hosts a separate website for each country and tailors its sites to different communities. In the USA, it has websites for children, Me Encanta for Spanish speakers, 365Black for African Americans, and a site for the Asian-Pacific American community.

The public can have a two-way conversation with the restaurant giant through all major social media sites in different countries. But McDonald's has experienced some difficulties with social media. The company has been criticized for simply putting out advertising rather than providing the useful, interesting content that fans expect from social media. Also, on Twitter, it receives lots of negative mentions focusing on the unhealthiness of its core products, a major issue for McDonald's.

Clever marketing to hungry drivers in Minnesota, USA.

Business Matters
Promotion

Promotion falls into two main categories:

1. Adverts: on TV, at the cinema, online, posters, press and social media. These aim to make people aware of the product and feel positive about it.
2. Sales promotions: displays, direct mail, merchandising (selling goods linked to a popular movie or event), telemarketing (selling by phone), exhibitions and loyalty schemes. These focus on persuading people to buy the product, or buy more of it, and recommend it to others.

Surfing the Internet with a high-speed wireless connection at a McDonald's in San Francisco, USA.

Building the Brand

Market research

McDonald's carries out market research into its target customers, which it calls 'key audiences'. It explores what appeals to them at McDonald's so the company can advertise to them effectively. According to its findings:

- Parents: go to McDonald's to give the kids a treat
- Children: want to go because it's fun and they like the toys in Happy Meals
- Businesspeople: can eat a quick meal there during the day
- Teenagers: like the affordable Saver Menu and Wifi access.

fast food and obesity

In countries where people regularly eat fast food, the obesity rate has risen alarmingly. For example, in the USA and UK, childhood obesity rates have more than tripled since 1980. In newer fast-food markets, including China and Japan, obesity is on the increase.

Is McDonald's to blame? Many health experts believe it contributes towards the obesity crisis. Both the fat content and portion size of its food have risen. In the 1950s, just one burger size was on offer, but now, far larger portions are offered cheaply. The double quarter-pounder burger contains 500 per cent more hamburger meat than the original size. A serving of fries has increased by 250 per cent. For his 2009 documentary, *Supersize Me*, film-maker Morgan Spurlock lived on McDonald's food alone for a month and his health suffered badly from the high-fat, high-sugar content of the diet.

Some meals that customers think are good for them contain a lot of fat. Chicken nuggets were introduced in 1983. They appeared to be healthier than burgers because they were made from chicken rather than red meat. But the meat comes from factory-farmed chickens that are kept in small cages and grow fat. A portion of chicken today contains 50 per cent more calories than it did in 1970.

In response, McDonald's claims that people don't eat its meals frequently enough to damage their health. It says people have to make their own decisions about what they eat, and healthy options are always available. Yet most people choose a burger and fries at McDonald's and have no idea of the calorie content of their meals – few read the calorie information on the wrappers.

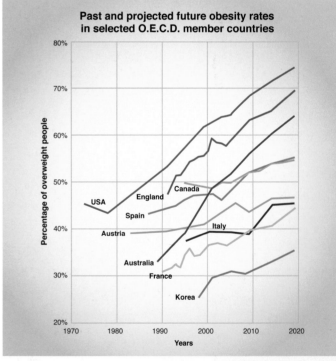

A 2010 graph from the Organization for Economic Cooperation and Development.

> **"** Evidence shows that if people are served larger portions, they'll eat larger portions! **"**

Kelly Brownell, Director of Yale University's Rudd Center for Food Policy and Obesity

Morgan Spurlock put on weight and suffered liver damage while eating McDonald's food alone.

Business Matters
Responding to criticism

Companies may make changes to their products in response to negative publicity. After Morgan Spurlock's documentary, McDonald's scrapped its 'supersize' portions and to date, they have not been brought back.

countering the health critics

Dan Coudreaut
Head of Culinary Innovation (from 2004)

Known as 'Chef Dan', Dan Coudreaut is in charge of developing new menu items for McDonald's. He's the brains behind dishes such as the Southwest salad, made with fire-roasted corn, savoury black beans, poblano peppers, tortilla strips and lime. To cater to the popular habit of grazing – having five small meals rather than three larger ones – he developed the snack wrap, with beef or chicken wrapped in a soft tortilla. All of Chef Dan's new recipes have to be easy for crews to make in the restaurants. Not all McDonald's innovations are successful though. There have been some famous failures, such as the McPizza, which flopped badly because it took too long to bake.

McDonald's has made efforts to offer customers healthier options such as fresh salads and low-fat desserts alongside its traditional burgers, fries and Coke.

The company still focuses on marketing to children because families form a large part of the customer base. But Happy Meals now include a child-sized portion of fries; fruit or yogurt; and fruit juice or milk instead of Coke. The website does not promote fries to children – it advertises fruity treats, such as the Pineapple Stick, made from 100 per cent pineapple.

Another venture is McCafé. Introduced in 2009, this adult-orientated McDonald's coffee bar focuses on coffees and fruit smoothies rather than fast food and offers lower prices than coffee chains Starbucks and Costa.

McDonald's states that it aims to include more fruit and vegetables in its menu and less salt, sugar and unhealthy fats. There is evidence that McDonald's is ahead of rival burger chains in this goal. Yet as obesity expert Kelly Brownell comments, McDonald's still offers a 'tidal wave of bad food with a few drops of goodness'.

Business Matters
Research and Development (R&D)

The food industry continually needs to innovate to keep up with eating trends. The R&D departments of food companies carry out market research to investigate consumers' eating habits and develop new menu items they believe will be popular.

workers and the environment

Battery chickens in cramped conditions, barely able to move.

" The production of much of the raw products which go into McDonald's meals, from burger patties to sauces, is subcontracted to different suppliers, making it impossible to assess the company in terms of a single golden standard. "

Peter Salisbury, Global Research, 2014

As well as being criticized for its unhealthy foods, McDonald's has been blamed for treating its staff badly and harming the environment. In the USA, for example, many frontline fast-food workers earn very low salaries. In the UK, 90 per cent of McDonald's staff work on 'zero hours' contracts – they only find out at the start of each week how many hours they will work.

McDonald's doesn't take criticism lightly. Between 1994–7, the company sued UK environmental activists Helen Steel and Dave Morris for distributing leaflets denouncing the company. The pair were unable to prove all their claims against McDonald's, but the judge eventually agreed that it exploited children, falsely said its food was nutritious (good for you), indirectly sponsored cruelty to animals and paid low wages. This was a blow to the brand.

Since the early 2000s, McDonald's has made progress in introducing ethical and eco-friendly practices. In the UK, burgers are now 100 per cent beef with no preservatives or added flavours. All fish in Filet-O-Fish and Fish Finger meals in Europe comes from sustainable fisheries.

Yet the advances are limited. The huge cattle herds that provide meat for McDonald's give off methane, which is a 'greenhouse gas'; it contributes to global warming. In the USA, cattle are often factory farmed – huge numbers are kept in crowded living conditions. Chickens are kept in a similar way in the UK.

McDonald's does not control where its meat and other supplies come from because 80 per cent of outlets are run by franchisees. The franchisees have to follow the laws of the countries they're based in, and some countries don't have tough rules to protect the environment. So whether McDonald's suppliers are eco-friendly or not depends on the country.

McDonald's crew busy at work in Beijing, China.

Business Matters
Eco-friendly efforts

It's important for the reputation of big brands to try to be more eco-friendly. For example, 80 per cent of McDonald's packaging is recycled.

hamburgers forever

McDonald's has proved highly successful in China.

Around 2000, McDonald's experimented with buying other kinds of food outlets, including Donatos Pizza and Pret A Manger. But it sold them again within a few years. In the future, McDonald's is likely to stick to its core business – as Chief Executive Officer Donald Thompson states, it's a hamburger chain and it always will be.

Having over-extended itself in the past, the company is wary of expanding too quickly. But it's likely to continue to grow in international markets, particularly in China, where it already has around 2,000 restaurants, and in African countries too.

McDonald's will have to cope with competition, particularly from 'fast casual' chains, such as Subway, Five Guys and Chipotle, which offer a healthier, fresher, more varied menu. To counter this, the company plans to invest in remodelling its stores and introducing mobile ordering and payments.

To stay ahead of its rivals, McDonald's will keep an eye on people's changing eating habits and their economic situation and alter products accordingly. It will be sure to offer plenty of value options for cash-strapped customers. The menu has grown by 70 per cent since 2007, and franchisees say this creates more work and costs, so it's likely the range of items will be reduced. Salads and fruit desserts will always be available but most customers will no doubt continue to visit McDonald's for the all-American meal of burgers, fries and Coke.

Business Matters
Cross selling

Cross selling is encouraging a customer who has already bought an item to buy another one – for example, the famous McDonald's sales line: 'Do you want fries with that?' It is effective if the salesperson suggests an item that goes well with the customer's original choice.

Fast-food outlets are growing in popularity in the Middle East – this McDonald's is in Dubai, United Arab Emirates.

Five Guys is one of the USA's fastest growing burger chains, and runs on a similar franchising system to McDonald's.

Building the Brand

McDonald's in the Middle East

In many Middle Eastern countries, people resent the influence of US culture but McDonald's has succeeded in adapting its message to show that the company respects local customs. Muslims do not eat meat from pigs, so in those countries, McDonald's uses no pork or ham. All meat is halal, from animals that have been killed in the Islamic way. In Oman, the Share Box is sold for families, to fit with the Middle Eastern tradition of sharing food from a central dish.

market a new McDonald's line

When you create a fantastic new product, you need to come up with a marketing strategy to sell it. Here's a sample marketing strategy for a possible line. Why not see if you can come up with your own idea for a new McDonald's menu item?

McTea Time

Following on from the development of McCafé, McDonald's can exploit the popularity of tea drinking in many countries and bring in new customers who do not normally eat at McDonald's.

Stage 1 Work out your objectives

Step 1: Make sure they fit with your corporate strategy.
Selling tea along with low-fat and low-sugar treats fits with McDonald's strategy to offer healthier items.

Step 2: What do you hope to achieve?
Research shows that many people prefer to graze on five smaller meals; the tea-time offering will bring in customers for another meal at McDonald's.

Stage 2 Product detail

Step 1: Product description and positioning
What is it?
A variety of teas will be offered, including traditional teas and herbal alternatives, accompanied by low-fat, low-sugar and gluten-free cookies and snacks.

Who is it for?
Target customers will be people who may not be attracted by the regular McDonald's menu but are looking for a low-priced venue for light refreshments.

What's the benefit?
The McTea Time menu provides a healthier alternative to high-sugar soft drinks.

Evidence to support your claims
The successful introduction of McCafé indicates there is a market for hot drinks and snacks.

Step 2: How will it be different from other products?
Light, tea-time treats not on the current McCafé or dessert menu will be introduced.

Step 3: What is the pricing policy?
As for McCafé, tea prices will be lower than at competitors' cafés such as Starbucks and Costa. The mark-up on tea (extra amount charged, above the cost of making it) served in cafés is very high so even with a lower price, the venture will still be profitable.

Step 4: What's the USP?
McTea Time will be available throughout opening hours at a lower price than rival cafés.

Stage 3 Understand the market
Step 1: Work out which niche gives the best sales possibilities
McTea Time will be launched first in markets where the tea-drinking habit is well established.

Step 2: Create customer profiles
Market research will identify groups that currently do not tend to go to McDonald's but could be encouraged to make use of the McTea Time offer.

Stage 4 Check the competition
What competition is there likely to be?
There are many established café chains as well as independent tea shops. McDonald's would need to offer good value to attract customers away from its rivals.

Stage 5 Build your sales plan
Step 1: Key messages
The key message will focus on the low price and the convenience of McTea Time, and the healthy accompanying snacks.

Step 2: Promotion
The promotion strategy will include advertising in traditional media – the press, TV, cinemas and billboards. The public relations team will offer features about McTea Time on its website and a huge social media and mobile marketing campaign will be rolled out. Promotions to engage customers will include 'tea try-outs' with vouchers for free teas and snacks.

Stage 6 Launch!
High-profile launch events will be held in all key target markets, with free teas for customers on launch day.

glossary

alliance
In business, an agreement between two companies to work together for the benefit of both of them.

assembly line
A line of workers and machines carrying out a process – each worker does their part of the job and passes the product on to the next person in the line.

augmented reality
A view of a real-world environment, with elements added by computer-made sound, video or graphics.

brand
A type of product made by a particular company.

calorie
A unit for measuring how much energy food will produce.

chain
A group of shops or restaurants owned by the same company.

Communism
The system of government in the former Soviet Union (1922–91), under which the state controlled the means of producing everything.

ethical
Morally right – in business it means treating people, animals and the environment well.

franchising/franchisee
Permission given by a company to somebody who wants to sell its goods or services in a particular area; the person who runs the business is called a franchisee.

frontline
In a restaurant, the people who work directly with customers.

global warming
The rise in temperature of the Earth's atmosphere that is caused by the increase of gases such as carbon dioxide and methane.

innovation
The introduction of new things, ideas or ways of doing something.

invest
To put money into a business in the hope of making a profit.

logo
A printed design or symbol that a company or an organization uses as its special sign.

loss
When a business loses money instead of making it.

marketing
Presenting, advertising and selling a company's products in the best possible way.

obesity
Being very overweight, in a way that is not healthy.

outlet
A shop or restaurant that sells goods made by a particular company or of a particular type.

preservative
A substance used to prevent food from decaying.

promotion
Activities done in order to increase the sales of a product or service.

publicity
The business of attracting the attention of the public to something, such as a new product.

reputation
The opinion that people have about something, such as a product, based on what has happened in the past.

slogan
A word or phrase that is easy to remember, often used in advertising to attract people's attention or to suggest an idea quickly.

sustainable
Involving the use of natural products and energy in a way that does not harm the environment.

'zero hours' contract
When a company does not employ workers for a fixed number of hours per week but tells them each week how many hours they will work.

further information

Books

For older children (12+)
Chew on This: Everything You Don't Want to Know about Fast Food
by Eric Schlosser (Puffin, 2006)

Grinding It Out: The Making of McDonald's
by Ray Kroc
(St Martin's Paperbacks, 2012)

Web

McDonald's abroad
http://content.time.com/time/world/article/0,8599,1932839,00.html

Fast Food Factory
www.bbc.co.uk/worldservice/specials/1616_fastfood/index.shtml

Happy Meals
www.happymeal.com/en_US/index.html

Marketing at McDonald's
www.mcdonalds.co.uk/content/dam/McDonaldsUK/People/
Schools-and-students/mcd_marketing.pdf

McDonald's
www.mcdonalds.co.uk

Videos

Big Mac: Inside the McDonald's Empire
www.youtube.com/watch?v=J4a4r-Iyf10

Ray Kroc Documentary McDonald's History
www.youtube.com/watch?v=k7bivuNlbi0

Supersize Me – selected scenes
www.youtube.com/watch?v=N2diPZOtty0&spfreload=10

A
adverts 14, 15, 18
apps 17
assembly-line production 10

B
Bergold, Roy, 17
Big Mac 4, 11, 13
brand 18
brand recognition 4
BrandZ 18
Brazil 4
breakfast 8
Burger King 10, 11

C
calories 4
charity 9
Chief Executive Officer, 9, 26
children 5, 14–15, 17, 19, 22
cleanliness 7, 9
Coca-Cola 17
Coudreaut, Dan 22
cross selling 26

D
direct marketing 18
Disney 17
diversification 4

E
eco-friendly 25
Egg McMuffin 8, 13
employees 4 *see also* staff

F
factory farming 20, 24–25
fat 4, 14, 20, 22
franchising/franchisees 10, 12–13, 25, 26, 27

G
GOL! 16–17
Golden Arches 5, 8, 9

H
Happy Meals 8, 14, 15, 17, 19, 22

K
Kroc, Ray 4, 6, 7, 8, 9, 10, 12

L
logo 5, 8, 9

M
market research 19, 23, 29
marketing 8, 14, 15, 17, 18, 22, 28–29
marketing alliances 16–17, 18
Mcdonald, Mac and Dick 6
McCafé 12, 22, 23, 28–29
media 18, 29

O
obesity 4, 17, 20–21, 22
owner/operators 10, 12

P
penetration 6
pricing tactics 6
product life cycle 11
profits 17
promotion 14, 18, 29

R
research and development (R&D) 23

Ronald McDonald 15
Ronald McDonald House 9

S
Saver Menu 19
sales (figures) 4
self-service 6, 10
Skinner, Jim 9
social media 18, 29
Spurlock, Morgan 20, 21
staff 9, 12, 25
Supersize Me 20

T
toys 8, 14, 17, 19
training 12
Turner, Fred 13
Twitter 18

W
Wifi 19
World Cup 16–17

Z
zero hours contracts 25

First published in Great Britain in 2015 by Wayland

Copyright © Wayland, 2015

All rights reserved.
Dewey Number: 338.7'6164795-dc23
ISBN: 978 0 7502 9255 9
Ebook ISBN: 978 0 7502 9256 6
10 9 8 7 6 5 4 3 2 1
Printed in China

Wayland
An imprint of Hachette Children's Group
Part of Hodder & Stoughton
Carmelite House
50 Victoria Embankment
London EC4Y 0DZ
An Hachette UK Company
www.hachette.co.uk
www.hachettechildrens.co.uk

Editor: Elizabeth Brent
Designer: Grant Kempster

Picture Credits: Cover: tehcheesiong/Shutterstock.com (left), Bikeworldtravel.Shutterstock.com (right); p4: Boris-B/Shutterstock.com; p5: Stefan Chabluk (top), 360b/Shutterstock.com (bottom); p6: Photoshot; p7: Everett Collection/REX (bottom), Art Shay/The LIFE Images Collection/Getty Images (top); p8: BikeWorldTravel/Shutterstock.com (top), tehcheesiong/Shutterstock.com (bottom); p9: Photoshot/TopFoto (top), hans engbers/Shutterstock.com (bottom); p10: H. Armstrong Roberts/ClassicStock/Topfoto; p11: Stefan Chabluk (top); Everett Collection/REX (bottom); p12: Action Press/ REX; p13: Alexanderphoto7 (top), Mark Peterson/Corbis (bottom left), Photoshot; p14: iStock/EdStock (left), Paisan Homhuan (right); p15: The Image Works/TopFoto; p16: Neilson Barnard/Getty Images for McDonald's; p17: Kurita KAKU/Gamma-Rapho via Getty Images; p18: iStock/skhoward; p19: Justin Sullivan/

Getty Images; p20: Stefan Chabluk; p21: Jakub Cejpek/Shutterstock.com (top), Snap Stills/REX (bottom); p22: Daniel Acker/Bloomberg via Getty Images; p23: Boris-B/Shutterstock.com; p24: branislavpudar/Shutterstock.com (left), Creative Nature Media/Shutterstock.com (right); p25: American Spirit/Shutterstock.com; p26: dailin/Shutterstock.com; p27: Michael Luhrenberg/iStock (top), Ken Wolter/Shutterstock.com (bottom); p28: saknakorn/Shutterstock.com; p29: Africa Studio/Shutterstock.com

The author would like to acknowledge these sources:

P5 map adapted from www.indexmundi.com/blog/wp-content/uploads/2013/02/macdonalds-worldwide.png;
P11 pie chart from www.wikinvest.com/stock/McDonald's_Corporation_(NYSE:MCD), 2012
P20 Graph from OECD, 2010

DISCOVER THE INCREDIBLE STORIES OF THE BUSINESSES BEHIND THESE WORLD-FAMOUS BRANDS

978 0 7502 9264 1

978 0 7502 9261 0

978 0 7502 9252 8

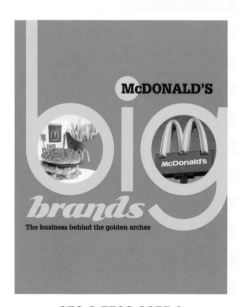

978 0 7502 9255 9